_____

Your name

1

This book is in memory of

_____

*Draw a picture of your special person
or paste their picture here.*

Each one of us
is a part of nature

and that includes children
and trees and flowers
and dogs and cats
and the wind and stars
and everything else
that exists.

4

When the leaves die in the fall,
their colors flash in the sunlight
as they gently tumble
from the trees.

We burn these dead leaves
or allow them to slowly
crumble into small pieces.
They become the earth
from which beautiful flowers
grow in the spring.

Each falling leaf is a tiny part
of the natural flow from birth
to death which happens
to all life forms.

This is the way
that life renews itself.
Death is necessary to life —
they go together.

We are all part of this flow.

EVERY LIVING CREATURE
DIES SOME DAY —

dogs and cats
birds and plants
also moms and dads
and grandparents.

Parts of us are dying all the time — like our hair and toenails.

Sometimes dying doesn't hurt anymore than a haircut because it is a very natural thing.

Other times dying does hurt the person we love.

It is okay for us to feel sad because we can't stop the pain.

Even the happy snowman
melts when summer comes
— and we miss him.

The body of the snowman melts back into the water from which he came just as the leaves turn back into the dirt from which the tree grew.

When we die, our bodies also slowly crumble and become part of the soil from which new plants grow.

We help this process happen by burying dead bodies in the ground or burning them into ashes.

This doesn't hurt even a little bit because the person no longer lives in the body.

When people and animals die,
they stop breathing and thinking.

Their hearts stop beating and
they no longer feel anything.

Death occurs when the very
special dancing flame of life
leaves the body and
does not return.

Sleep is good for us.
We sleep every night and
always wake up in the morning.

Death is not like sleep.
Dead people don't wake up.

Good morning!

Most people live a long
time and don't die until
their bodies wear out —

but some people are killed
in accidents like when
their car crashes —

and still other people
get very sick and die.

Sick or hurt people
usually get well again
because our bodies are very
good at healing themselves.

But sometimes the body is too
damaged to ever work right again.
Not even the doctors and nurses
can make the body healthy.

When death happens, we have to say goodbye. Sometimes this makes us feel sad.

How do you feel about saying goodbye?

People often gather to say a final goodbye before the body is buried or burned.

A funeral is when family and friends come together and remember the good things about the dead person.

Sometimes the dead body is there to see or to touch if anyone wants to.

CASKET

Please draw a face showing how you feel about the death of someone special.

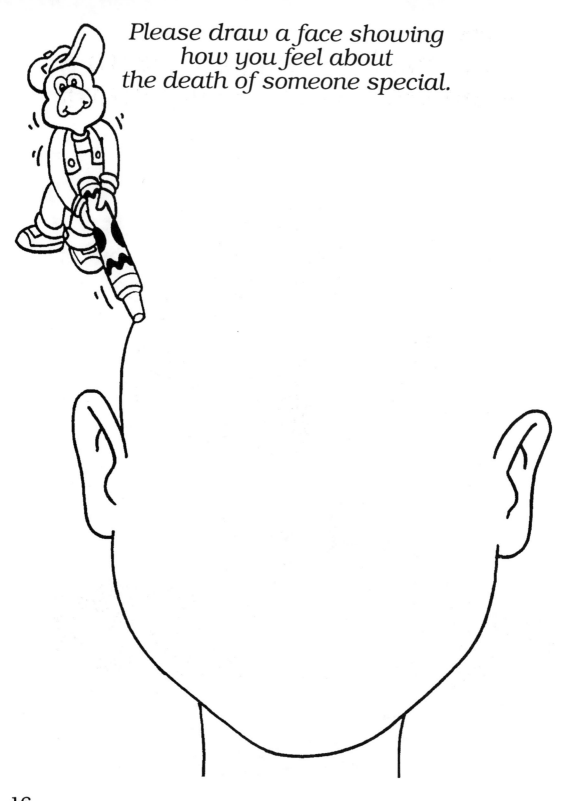

Some kids laugh at death
— pretending to be very brave.

Naa! Naa!
You can't hurt me.

Other kids, like me, are afraid of death.

We run as fast as we can to get away — and that is okay.

Death can seem very scary.

What do you do when you are afraid?

The one thing that we can't do is HIDE from death and pretend that it doesn't exist.

Where do you go when you want to hide out?

Death is like an elephant. It is much too big and important to ignore.

Why can't we ignore death?

Even if we know that death
is a natural part of living,
we are often very sad
when a loved one dies.

We may feel like we can never
laugh again.

Sometimes we feel guilty when a loved one dies — like maybe we should have been nicer to them — or maybe we did something that caused them to die — or maybe we could have saved them.

The wise owl knows this is not true and so do you.

We may feel mad when someone
special dies and that is okay.
We miss them very much.

It is also okay to be happy when a
loved one dies because they no
longer feel pain.

It is especially okay to cry and cry.
The tears help to wash away the pain.

Please draw a picture of death.

Sometimes it does not seem fair that a loved one dies while other people still live.

It helps a little to remember that everyone is special to someone and all of us lose people that we love.

It may help you to feel better if you talk about your feelings with someone you trust.

They will understand.

Who can you talk to about your feelings?

When a person dies,
they continue to live through the
things that they leave behind —
like the flowers they have planted,
the people they have helped, and
the words they have written.

Our loved ones also continue to
live in our memories.

*What are some memories you have
of a dead or dying loved one?*

_____

_____

_____

_____

_____

_____

_____

_____

_____

Leaves die,
but the tree still stands.

Trees die,
but the forest remains.

Everywhere there is death,
there is also birth.

Each spring
the trees sprout new leaves,
flowers push through the soil
to burst into bloom,
while kittens and puppies
play in the fields.

The miracle of life is everywhere
and it will continue
for your children and
your children's children.

Please draw a picture of life

Each person experiences life
and death in a different way.
There are many questions for which
we do not have clear answers.

Your family and counselors will
know much more about these
things — this is a good time
to ask questions and
tell them how you feel.

Remember that you are never
alone. Your family, teachers, and
friends are always there for you.

They love you very much and
that love does not die —
LOVE IS FOREVER.

This is a good time to write a letter saying goodbye.

Dear _____ ,

Remember when you and I were together and

_____ ?

It was fun the time when you _____

_____.

I wish we had _____

_____.

I feel _____

because _____

_____.

I hope _____.

Thank you for _____

_____.

Signed _____